# THE DRIVING BOOK FOR TEENS

---

LEARN TO DRIVE - MASTER DEFENSIVE DRIVING SKILLS, ROAD SIGNS, AND DMV WRITTEN TEST QUESTIONS

OLIVIA SUMMERVILLE

# INTRODUCTION

Learning how to drive is exciting — and maybe a little nerve-wracking (especially for your parents, lol.)

Getting your driver's license means that you'll have more independence and freedom to do the things that you want to do. It's an important step in your journey to becoming an adult and achieving your dreams in life.

However, driving also comes with a lot of responsibility.

Most people take it for granted, but ***driving is one of the most dangerous things that people do every day***.

I'm not trying to scare you or add to your anxiety, but I do want you to understand that driving carelessly, or without fully understanding the rules of the road can have deadly consequences.

The good news is that you can become a safe driver by learning a few simple driving skills and knowing what to do if you find yourself in an emergency situation.

The goal of this book is to make learning the rules of the road simple and straightforward.

We've broken this book into five sections to make it easy for you to learn how to drive and to use this book as a reference guide if you are studying for the DMV written exam.

**Section 1** covers the basics of safe driving, as well as some of the most common causes of car accidents and how to avoid them.

We also created a simple checklist of things that you should do before you drive to make sure that you don't run into any trouble when you're out on the road.

**Section 2** teaches you all of the essential driving skills that you need to know before you start driving.

These are things like passing, parallel parking, and what to do in common emergency situations.

After reading about the different driving skills, we highly recommend practicing them with a parent, adult, or driving instructor as often as you can.

**Section 3** covers basic driving laws that every driver needs to know, like what to do if you get pulled over and get a ticket.

**Section 4** contains all of the different traffic lights and road signs that you might encounter when driving.

**Section 5** has 40 practice questions and explanations to help you test your knowledge of safe driving practices.

You can review the questions on your own or have a parent or friend quiz you.

Let's get started!

# SECTION 1: SAFE DRIVING BASICS

# HOW TO AVOID A CRASH

In this section, you are going to learn the most common causes of fatal car crashes and what you can do to avoid them.

---

## Cell Phones

I know, I know. You've probably been lectured about not using your phone while driving a billion times already, but hear me out.

If you're like most teens, your life revolves around your phone. It's natural to want to check it whenever you get a social media notification or hear the "ding" of a text alert.

These devices are designed to make the impulse to check your phone uncontrollable.

Essentially, we're all brainwashed, lol!

The problem is that driving requires your FULL ATTENTION.

Things can change on the road in a matter of seconds and you need to be able to respond quickly.

If you're reading or responding to a message while driving, your chances of getting into a fatal accident go up exponentially because you won't be able to fast enough.

Here are a couple of tips to manage your phone use while driving:

1. **Turn off social media and text notifications.** By turning off notifications, you won't feel the impulse to check your phone while driving because you won't hear the "ding" or see the pop-up when you get a new message.

2. **Turn off your phone, or put it on "airplane" mode when you're behind the wheel**. This might not be practical for everyone, especially if you need to use a navigation app for directions, but it will help you break the habit of compulsively checking your phone if that's a problem for you.

3. **Use "smart assistants" to make calls while driving.** Most phones today have voice-activated calling features like Siri or Google Assistant. Instead of looking through your contacts if you need to make a call, say "*Hey Siri*" or "*Hey Google, call so-and-so.*"

4. **Pull over if you need to respond to a message.** If you absolutely must read or respond to a text or email, find a safe place to pull over and stop. Never read or respond to messages while the car is moving.

5. **Get a dash-mounted holder for your phone.** Putting your phone in a holder keeps you from fumbling around with it while you're driving. It also makes it easy to see where you're going if you're using a GPS app for directions.

**Driving When You're Tired**

Driving when you haven't had enough sleep is incredibly dangerous. When you're tired, your ability to think and react slows way down. You're also at risk of falling asleep while driving.

If you feel drowsy, avoid driving if you can.

If you are on a long car ride, roll down the windows or turn on the air conditioner to bring in cool, fresh air. Pullover if you need to and get some rest before continuing on.

As a last resort, you can grab a cup of coffee or a caffeinated beverage to help you stay awake and alert, but you shouldn't rely on caffeine all the time because this can affect your health negatively over the long term.

**Distractions**

Anything that takes your attention off the road while you are driving increases your odds of getting into an accident.

*Here are some common distractions to avoid:*

- Eating
- Putting on makeup
- Searching for items in the car
- Getting distracted by pets or other passengers
- Frequently changing music or other media.

Safe Driving Tip: Create a playlist *before* you start driving, or use voice commands to change the songs. Some steering wheels also have controls that let you change songs and adjust the volume without taking your hands off the wheel.

### Medications

If you start taking a new medication, always ask your doctor or pharmacist if it can affect your ability to drive. You can also read the information that comes with your medication to learn about possible side effects.

**It is your responsibility to know how your medications affect your ability to drive safely.**

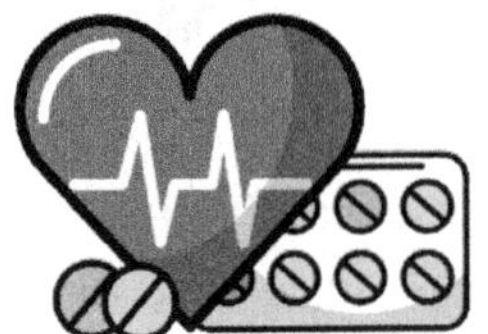

Remember, it's not only prescription medications that can impair your ability to drive. Some over the counter cold and allergy medications can also make you drowsy and impair your ability to stay alert.

### Driving Under the Influence

Here's another one that I'm sure you've heard a thousands time before, but it's important, like *really, really* important…

It is NEVER *safe* to drive if you have been drinking or taking drugs. Both drugs and alcohol impair your vision, judgment, and ability to react quickly.

As a teen, there may be times when you feel pressured to drink or take substances that can impair your ability to drive. Peer pressure is a real thing and it can be difficult to say "no."

If you find yourself in a situation like this, keep in mind that there are always consequences for bad decisions.

Aside from getting into an accident, injuring or killing yourself and others, you could also lose your license, be forced to pay a big fine, or face prison time.

All it takes is one bad decision to mess up the rest of your life. This might sound dramatic, but it's something you really need to think about and take seriously so that you can make good decisions.

***What do to if…***

I never condone illegal behavior, *however*, I was also a teenager once and sometimes we don't always make the best choices.

If you are in a situation where you have been drinking or using substances, ***do not drive***.

**Here are some alternatives that could save your life:**

- Call a friend to come pick you up.

- Call a parent or family member. *Yes, you might get into trouble, but it's better than getting seriously injured in an accident or killing an innocent person.*
- Stay where you are until you're sober and able to drive safely.
- Use public transportation or call a ride share service like Uber if it's available in your area.

### Carbon Monoxide

Carbon monoxide is an invisible, poisonous gas that is produced by your car's exhaust system.

If you inhale too much of it, it can make you sleepy, lose consciousness, or even kill you.

You can reduce the risk of carbon monoxide poisoning by not running the engine in a garage when the door is closed, or opening your car windows when you are parked outside with the engine running.

You should have your exhaust system checked regularly for leaks. If your exhaust system is leaking into the main cabin of the vehicle it could effect your ability to drive and harm your health.

# BE PREPARED FOR ANYTHING

Driving a car might seem as simple as getting in and turning on the engine, but there are a lot of things that can go wrong when you're out on the road.

Being prepared by keeping a few essential items in the car will give you peace of mind and ensure that you can handle challenging situations if you need to.

Here is a list of things that you can do to be prepared for the most common emergency situations you may encounter while driving.

### 1. Phone Charger or Battery Pack

If you have car trouble or get into a minor accident, you'll want to be able to call someone for help. But you can't do that if your cell phone battery dies.

Always keep an extra phone charger in the car so that you can plug in your phone if you need to.

You may also want to get a battery pack that you can use to charge your phone in case you are unable to start your car.

**2. List of Emergency Contacts**

If you run into trouble, you should have list of people or local services that you can call for help.

For example, look up phone numbers for local towing companies or AAA (if you are a member) and add them to your contacts in your phone.

You can also write these contacts down on a piece of paper and keep a copy in your glove compartment.

**3. Tire Repair Kit**

One of the most common emergencies that drivers face when they're out on the road is getting a flat tire.

If you subscribe to a roadside assistance service like AAA, you can call to have someone fix your tire for you.

However, if you do not have this service, you can easily fix the tire yourself if you have the proper items on hand.

**Here are the items you should have in your tire repair kit:**

- Spare tire
- Car jack
- Tire iron for removing bolts
- Air pump

You might also want to keep an old blanket, gloves, or a towel in your trunk to put down while you're working.

You can also keep a can of "*fix-a-flat*" in your car. This is a product that can be purchased at most gas stations. It injects foam into your flat tire. Once it hardens, it will seal the leak and you can drive a short distance to have the tire changed at another location.

**4. Car Battery Kit**

Another common car emergency is having a dead battery. This can happen if you leave your lights on too long while the car is off. It can also happen in cold weather if your battery needs to be replaced.

Keeping a set of jumper cables or a portable car battery charger in your trunk will ensure that you are able to start your car if your battery dies.

**5. Ice Scraper**

If you live in a region where it snows frequently, you should keep an ice scraper in your car.

This will allow you to remove snow and ice from your windows quickly.

**6. Roadside Emergency Kit**

If your car breaks down on the side of a road or highway, you should place warning signs such as road flairs or hazard signs behind your vehicle so that it is easier for oncoming traffic to see you. If you have called a tow truck driver or AAA, this will also make it easier for the driver to find you.

You can find roadside emergency kits online or in most large retail or auto parts stores.

### 7. First Aid Kit

Finally, it's a smart idea to keep a basic first aid kit in your car in case of an emergency.

This can helpful if you get into a minor accident or need to treat an injury while waiting for help to arrive.

# DRIVING CHECKLIST

There are certain things that you should always do before you drive that will help keep you safe when you are out on the road.

Here's a list of all the things that you should do before you turn on the car.

We recommend referring to this checklist every time you drive, until these steps become a habit.

### 1. Check Your Tires

Before you get in the car, take a quick walk around the vehicle and look at each of your tires. Do any of them look low or flat?

This step is important because it can prevent you from getting a flat tire or having a blowout when you're out on the road.

If one of your tires looks low, use an air pump to inflate them to the correct

PSI (for most cars, this is 30-35 PSI, but your check your car's manual if you're not sure.)

If you don't have an air pump at home, drive to the nearest gas station if you can. Most gas stations have an air pump that you can use for free or for a small fee.

You should check your tire pressure ***at least once a month*** or before going on a long car trip.

**2. Are Your Windows Clean?**

Dirt, dust, and mud can impair your ability to see clearly. If your windshield or side windows are dirty, be sure to clean them off before you start driving.

If your car is covered with snow or ice, you must clean and defrost all windows before you drive. You can do this with an ice scraper and/or your car's defroster.

**3. Check Fluid Levels**

Before you drive, you should always check the following fluid levels:

- Gas (or battery for electric vehicles)
- Windshield washer fluid
- Engine oil

You should also have your brake and transmission fluid checked regularly. See a mechanic or look inside your car's manual if you do not know how to check these on your own.

. . .

**Car Tip**: If you live in a region where the temperature falls below freezing, make sure that your gas tank is always at least 1/4 full. If let your gas level get too low in cold temperatures, your gas line could freeze and your car won't start.

### 4. License, Insurance, & Registration

You should always have your driver's license (or permit), car registration, and insurance information with you whenever you drive.

If you are stopped for a traffic violation, or if you get into a collision, you will be asked to provide these documents.

Keep in mind that it is illegal to drive a car that is not registered or insured, so make sure that you have proof of registration and insurance in the car at all times.

### 5. Seat Belts for Everyone

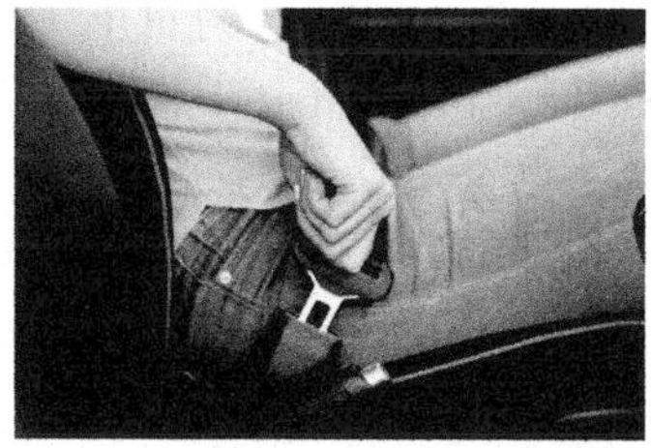

The first thing that you should do when you get in a car is put on your seat belt. This can save your life if you are in an accident.

It is illegal to drive or ride in a vehicle without wearing a seat belt. You will get a ticket and be required to pay a fine if you are pulled over.

You can also be held responsible for any passengers who are under the age of 18 who are not wearing a seatbelt in your car. Make sure everyone is buckled up before you drive.

The correct way to wear a seatbelt is to place the shoulder strap across your chest and ensure the lap belt is snug across your hips. Wearing your seatbelt incorrectly could cause serious injury if you are in a crash.

**6. Adjust Your Seat**

It is important to adjust your seat so that you can easily reach the pedals and see clearly out of the windshield.

You should sit ***at least 10 inches*** away from an airbag. If you sit too close, you could be seriously injured if you are in a crash.

**7. Adjust the Mirrors**

You should adjust the side and rearview mirrors every time you get into a vehicle so that you can see objects behind you.

When you adjust your side mirrors, you should be able to see what is to the side and rear of your car. The center rearview mirror is for viewing objects that are directly behind you.

**8. Headlights**

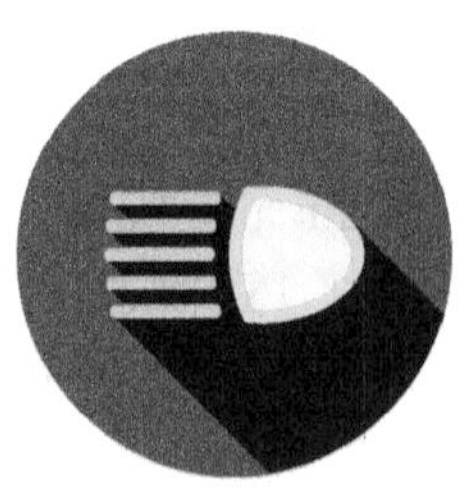

Is it dark or raining? If so, turn on your headlights.

In most states, you must turn on your low-bean headlights if you are driving after sunset or before sunrise.

**9. Glasses & Contacts**

If you have prescription glasses or contacts, you should always wear them when you are driving.

If you have prescription sunglasses, be sure to bring them with you when you drive during the daytime.

**10. GPS Navigation Apps**

Do you know where you're going? Do you need directions?

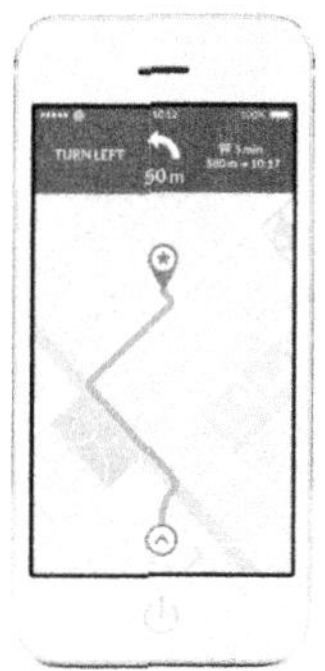


If you need to get directions from a GPS navigation app on your phone or other device, look up directions before you start driving.

It is recommended that you place your phone or GPS device in a dash holder or some other place where you can see it clearly.

***Never try to look up directions while you are driving.***

# SECTION 2: DRIVING SKILLS

## STEERING

Proper technique is important when steering your vehicle because it allows you to stay in control at all times.

**Hand Position**

If you think of the steering wheel as a clock, put your hands at nine o'clock and three o'clock.

Place your knuckles on the outside of the wheel and stretch your thumbs along the rim. This way if the airbag is deployed, it will reduce injury to your face, arms, and hands.

**Controlling the Vehicle**

While there isn't one correct way to steer a vehicle, here are a few methods that are recommended.

**Hand-to-Hand Steering**

This steering method is often called "***push/pull***."

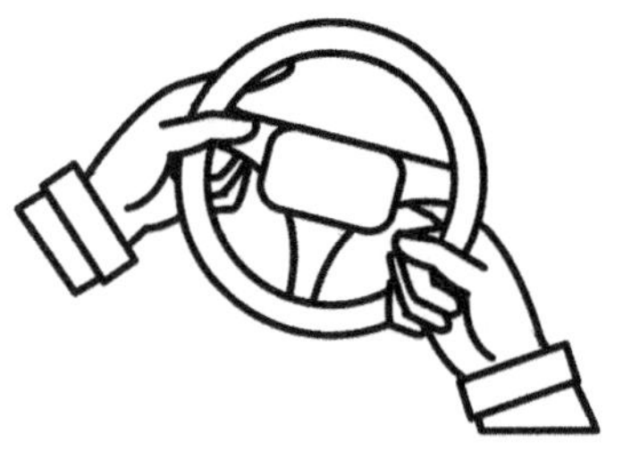

You start with your hands at 9 and 3 o'clock, or even lower at 8 and 4 o'clock.

When you turn the wheel, one hand pushes it up, while the other pulls it down.

**Hand-Over-Hand Steering**

This way of steering can be used when turning at low speeds, parking, or recovering from a skid.

When using this method, start with your hands at 9 and 3 o'clock.

One hand will push the wheel up while the other hand lets go and reaches across to grasp it and pull it downwards.

**One-Hand Steering**

The only time that a 12 o'clock hand position is recommended is when backing up while turning, since the driver must turn around in their seat to see where they are going.

## TURNING

Turning is an important driving skill. While it may seem basic, there are a number of situations that you may find confusing when first learning to drive.

In this section, we'll go over the different types of turns and how to perform each one safely.

**Left Turns**

To make a left turn, you should drive close to the center divider line or into the left turn lane.

1. Turn on your signal 100 feet before the turn.
2. Look over your left shoulder and slow down.
3. Stop behind the line marked on the pavement.
4. Look to your right and then to your left again before turning.
5. Make your turn without "cutting in" on another car's lane.

### Left turn from a two-way street

When you want to turn left onto a cross street, start in the left lane closest to the middle of the street.

Keep your wheels pointed straight ahead until it is safe to start your turn. If you are hit from behind, you could be pushed into oncoming traffic.

### Left turn from a two-way street onto a one-way street

When you want to turn left from a two-way street into a one-way street, start the turn from the lane closest to the middle of the street.

If there are no cars in your way, turn into any lane that is open.

### Left turn from a one-way street onto a one-way street

When you are driving on a one-way street, if there is another one-way street on the left side, you can turn left from the far left lane.

Watch out for people walking or riding bicycles because they have the right to use the turn lane too.

Turn into the nearest open lane.

### Right Turns

If you want to turn right, you should drive close to the right edge of the roadway before making your turn.

Watch out for bikes, pedestrians, or motorcycles as you approach the turn.

Stop before the limit line. Look both ways and make your turn when it is safe to do so.

**Making a right turn at a red light**

If you come to a red traffic light you must stop.

If there is no oncoming traffic, make sure that there is not a sign that says "NO *right turns on red.*"

If there is no sign prohibiting right turns on red you can make a "right on red" as long as you have enough space to complete the turn safely.

You may NOT make a right turn at a red arrow even if there is no oncoming traffic.

**Right Turn With a Dedicated Lane**

You do NOT have to stop if you turn onto a road with a non-merging lane that is dedicated to vehicles turning right.

You must follow any lights or signs that are in the lane for vehicles going straight through the intersection.

When driving near pedestrian crosswalks, always yield to pedestrians who may be crossing.

**Right turn from a one-way street onto a one-way street**

If you are turning right from a one-way street into another one-way street, start in the far right lane.

If it is safe, you can end your turn in any lane that is not blocked off. Sometimes signs or pavement markings will let you turn right from another lane.

**Turning at a "T" intersection from a one-way street onto a two-way street**

If you turn at a "T" intersection from a one-way street into a two-way street, look for traffic that has the right of way.

You can turn right or left from the center lane.

Watch for vehicles, motorcycles, and bicyclists inside your turn.

**U-Turns**

A "***U-turn***" is when you turn your car around 180 degrees to travel in the complete opposite direction.

Sometimes it is okay to make U-turns, while other times it is not. If U-turns are illegal in the area where you are driving, there will be a sign posted.

*Legal U-Turns*

You can make a U-turn if it is safe and legal. It is okay to make a U-turn in most residential areas.

To make a U-turn, turn on your signal and get in the far left lane or the center left-turn lane.

There should be no vehicles within 200 feet when you start your U-turn.

If you are at a traffic light with a green arrow protecting you from oncoming traffic, you can safely make a U-turn.

**Warning:** Watch out for people making a "right on red" at an intersection before starting your turn. They may not be aware that you intend to make a complete u-turn.

*Illegal U-Turns*

**NEVER** make a U-Turn in the following situations:

- at a railroad crossing
- on a divided highway when you have to cross a dividing section, curb, land, or two sets of double yellow lines.
- when you cannot see 200 feet in either direction because of a curve, hill, fog, etc.
- when you don't have enough room to make the turn without causing a crash.
- on a one-way street.
- in front of a fire station
- in high-traffic areas or business districts.

# MANAGING SPACE

In this section, you'll learn different techniques for managing the space around your vehicle when you're out on the road.

"*Managing space*" is a *defensive driving skill* where you leave enough room between you and the vehicles around you. This gives you time to react if another driver swerves or slams on the brakes.

### 1. Scanning

When driving, ***constantly scan your surroundings*** for potential dangers.

Look ahead **10 to 15 seconds**, look to the sides of your car, and check your mirrors often to see what's going on around you.

### 2. Following Distance

A safe following distance in good driving conditions is **4 seconds**.

Remember to allow more space when the road or weather conditions are not ideal.

***Tailgating***, or following too closely behind the car in front of you, is dangerous because it increases your chances of getting into a crash.

### 3. Blind Spots

A "*blind spot*" is an area around a vehicle that a driver can't see in their rearview or side mirrors.

You should avoid driving next to other vehicles on the highway. You could be in their blind spot and they may not see you.

### 4. Entering a Freeway or Highway

You should try to make room for cars entering the freeway *even if* you have the right-of-way.

When entering the freeway, you should drive ***at or near the same speed*** as the flow of traffic.

### 5. Changing Lanes

Always check to see what is behind you before changing lanes. There could be a vehicle in your blind spot.

Use your mirrors and turn your head to the side and glance back before moving into the lane.

Turn on your signal for ***5 seconds*** before moving into the new lane. This lets other drivers know what you intend to do.

### 6. Driving Near Parked Cars

You should not drive too close to parked cars if you can avoid it. They could open their door at any time.

### 7. Stopping

If you are going ***55 mph***, you will need ***400 feet*** of space to come to a complete stop.

If you are traveling ***35 mph***, you will need ***210 feet*** to come to a complete stop.

Note: When driving in poor weather conditions such as rain or fog, it takes longer to stop than when operating in perfect conditions.

### 8. Intersections

When you come to an intersection, you should ***look left, right, and then back to your left again*** before crossing, since traffic coming from the left will be closest to you.

***Never block an intersection.***

If you come to an intersection with a green light, but traffic is backed up and you don't have enough room to get across, wait to cross until you have enough space.

### 9. Signaling

Always use your turn signal when making a turn, changing lanes, or merging on or off the freeway.

If you are planning to make a turn, you should turn on your signal ***100 feet before the turn*** to let other drivers know that you are slowing down.

### 10. Backing Up

When backing up, ***turn your head*** so that you can see through the rear window. Never rely solely on your backup camera or mirrors.

## DRIVING LANES & LINES

In this section, you will learn the skill of lane control.

When you are out on the road you will see different types of lines or markings that let you know what you are allowed to do and what you are NOT allowed to do depending on the lane you are in.

Lane control lines, markings and signs let you know when you can:

- change lanes,
- pass,
- turn, or
- make other moves on the road.

Lane control lines are usually white or yellow.

They may be solid or broken.

It is important to pay attention to the type of line that is controlling the lane you are driving in and to understand what each type of line means.

Some highways and roadways may also use lights to indicate when a lane is open or what direction traffic is moving in.

These lights can change at anytime, so make sure that you stay alert and pay attention.

***Here are the different types of lane control lines and what they mean.***

**Two Solid Yellow Lines**

If you see two solid yellow lines you CANNOT pass.

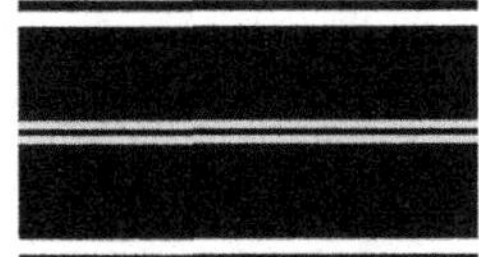

You must stay in your lane until the line closest to your lane changes to a broken line.

**Broken Yellow Lines**

If the yellow line closest to you is broken, you CAN pass if it is safe to do so.

However, cars traveling in the other direction may NOT pass if they have a solid yellow line.

Alternatively, if the yellow line closest to you is solid, that means that your lane is NOT allowed to pass.

**Two Sets of Solid Double Yellow Lines**

If you see two sets of double yellow lines, this should be treated as a barrier.

You should not drive over this barrier or make a turn across it unless there is a designated opening in the lines.

**Solid White Lines**

Solid white lines mark traffic lanes that are traveling in the same direction, such as one-way streets.

**Broken White Lines**

Broken white lines separate traffic lanes on roads with two or more lanes traveling in the same direction.

You can pass other vehicles traveling in the same direction by changing lanes on multi-lane highways.

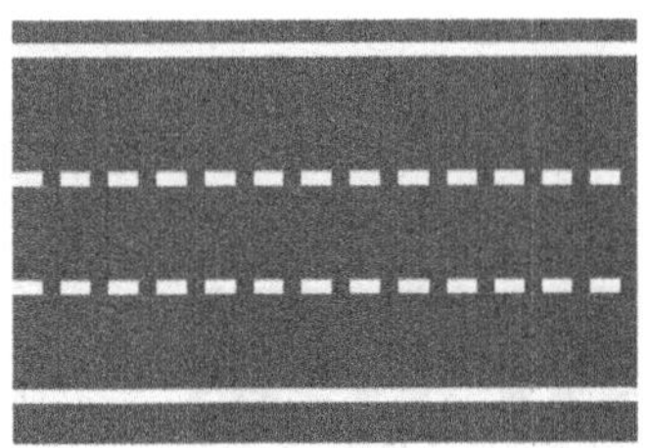

**Double White Lines**

When you see two solid white lines, this means there is a lane barrier.

You should not change lanes unless a single broken white line appears.

These are often seen on highways and off-ramps.

**Choosing a Lane**

Which lane should you use?

*3-Lane Highways*

If you are driving on a highway or freeway with three lanes traveling in one direction, you need to know that each lane is treated differently by drivers.

**Fast Lane** — The lane furthest to the left is typically called "***the fast lane***." Drivers use this lane to pass other cars.

**Slow Lane** —The lane furthest to the right is often referred to as "***the slow lane***" or "**exit lane**." Cars frequently merge onto the highway or exit from the right lane, therefore traffic tends to move slower.

It is recommended that slower-moving vehicles use the right lane so that other drivers can pass easily.

**Middle Lane** — The flow of traffic is usually the smoothest in ***the middle lane***.

If you intend to stay on the highway or freeway for several miles, it is recommended that you use the middle lane unless you need to pass (then use the left lane.)

If you need to drive slow for any reason or if your exit is coming up soon, use the right lane.

*2-Lane Roadways*

If there are two lanes traveling in your direction, the left lane is still considered the "*fast lane*" or "*passing lane*."

You should always drive in the right lane *unless* you are passing another car.

After passing, move back into the right lane when it is safe to do so.

Avoid weaving in and out of traffic. Stick to one lane as much as you can.

**Changing Lanes**

Changing lanes is when you move from one lane to another, or when you enter the freeway or exit onto another road.

Before changing lanes, make sure that there is enough room for your vehicle in the next lane.

Look behind and beside you before moving into the new lane to make sure no other cars are in the way.

Turn on your signal 5 seconds before you change lanes to let other drivers know where you intend to move.

**HOV or Carpool Lanes**

HOV or "High Occupancy Vehicle" lanes are for vehicles that carry a certain minimum number of passengers.

For example, if the posted minimum is two passengers, you may only enter the HOV lane if there is at least one other passenger in the car.

Signs at the onramp to the HOV lane or along the freeway will tell you the minimum number of people per vehicle required to enter the carpool lane.

These signs also list the days and times when the passenger requirement applies.

The pavement in this lane is marked with a ***diamond symbol*** *to let you know that you are approaching an HOV lane.*

You should NEVER cross over the double parallel solid lines to enter or exit an HOV lane. Only enter or exit at designated spots.

**Center Left Turn Lanes**

Center left-turn lanes are often located in the middle of a two-way street.

The middle lane can be used when you want to make a left turn or if you need to make a U-turn.

You can only drive for ***200 feet*** in the center left-turn lane. This type of lane should NOT be used as a regular traffic lane or as a passing lane.

**Turnout Areas and Lanes**

Some two-lane roads have designated places called "turnouts" where you can pull over to let faster moving cars pass if there is no designated passing lane.

You should drive into a turnout area if there are 5 or more vehicles following closely behind you. Once the vehicles have passed, you can continue driving on the road.

**End of Lane Markings**

If you see a broken line on the pavement, it means that the lane is ending.

If you are driving in this lane, be ready to exit the freeway or merge into another lane.

Road signs will tell you what to do next.

**Yield Lines**

Yield lines let you know that oncoming traffic has the right of way. They have white triangles across the lane of traffic. If a car is coming you should stop behind the yield line and wait until you have enough space to enter the road.

**Bicycle Lanes**

A bike lane is a road for bikes that is marked with pavement lines and signs. Sometimes bike lanes are painted green to make them more visible to drivers.

You can not drive in a designated bike lane unless you are parking, entering, or leaving the road.

**Types of Bike Lanes**

There are different types of bikes lanes that you may encounter while driving.

*Regular Bike Lanes*

A regular bike lane is set up on the side of a street next to the regular roadway that cars use.

The regular bike lane has a solid white line that changes into a dashed line when it approaches an intersection.

*Buffered Bike Lanes*

Buffered bike lanes provide more space between cars and cyclists. The lane is usually marked with a chevron symbol.

*Bike Routes*

Bike routes allow cyclists to ride on streets that cars also drive on. In this case, bikes do not have a designated lane. Rather, they must share the road with normal traffic.

You will see signs or markings telling you where the bike route is.

*Bicycle Boulevards*

Bicycle boulevards are a type of lane that is for bikes only.

They give bicyclists a safe and convenient route, without having to worry about sharing the lane with cars.

*Separated Bikeways*

Separated bikeways are similar to bike lanes, but they have a physical barrier that separates them from the street and vehicle traffic.

*Shared Roadway Bicycle Markings*

Shared roadway bicycle markings or "*sharrows*" are symbols on the street that let cars know that bikes are allowed to ride in the lane.

They also help bicyclists stay safe and in the correct lane position.

# PASSING

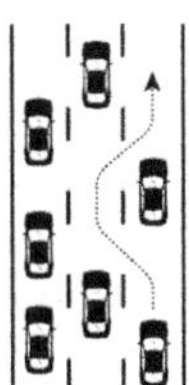

## Passing

As a general rule, you should always ***pass on the left***.

You may pass on the *right side* of a vehicle IF you are on a highway with two or more lanes traveling in the same direction.

When preparing to pass, you should turn on your signal **5-seconds** before moving out of your lane to pass.

You are only allowed to pass <u>one</u> vehicle at a time.

Before you return to your lane after passing, use your mirrors to make sure you have enough space.

NEVER pass if you are approaching a hill or curve that limits your visibility of oncoming traffic, or if you are within ***100 feet*** of an intersection, bridge, tunnel, or railroad crossing.

## SHARING THE ROAD

### Large Trucks

It takes large trucks ***longer to stop*** than smaller passenger vehicles.

If you slow down or stop quickly in front of a large truck, it could cause a collision.

Do NOT drive alongside a large truck unless you are passing. Tractor-trailers have bigger blind spots than regular cars. They may not be able to see you.

When long vehicles ***make turns***, the back wheels have ***a shorter path*** than those in the front. This causes them to have to swing out wide when turning.

### Safety Zones & Bus Stops

If you come to a safety zone where people are boarding or exiting a bus or trolley, you must stop and wait until all pedestrians are safely away from the road before you proceed.

## Railroad Crossings

Busses and trucks transporting ***hazardous materials*** must ALWAYS stop before crossing railroad tracks, regardless of whether there is a stop sign or signal.

NEVER stop on the railroad tracks for any reason.

When approaching a railroad crossing, look AND listen for oncoming trains.

NEVER assume there will be a signal or gate to warn you of an oncoming train.

Stop ***at least 15 feet*** (but no more than 50 feet) from the nearest railroad tracks when crossing devices, such as lights, are active or blinking.

## Emergency Vehicles

When an emergency vehicle is using their siren, you must pull over to the shoulder of the road and stop to give them room to get through.

NEVER stop in an intersection if an emergency vehicle is coming because they may need to make a turn.

NEVER follow an emergency vehicle to their destination.

It is illegal to drive within ***300 feet behind*** any emergency vehicle when its siren is on.

## Horse Drawn Vehicles

When driving near horse-drawn vehicles, use extra caution because the driver could lose control of the animal.

### Motorcycles

When driving behind a motorcycle, ***keep a 4-second following distance.*** This way, if the motorcycle stops suddenly or skids, you have a better chance of avoiding a collision.

### Bicycles

When passing a cyclist, you should ***leave at least 3 feet of space between you and them*** to avoid knocking them off their bike.

### Pedestrians

NEVER pass a vehicle that is stopped at a crosswalk. Someone could be crossing the street that you are not able to see.

If you come to a crosswalk where pedestrians are waiting to cross, stop before you reach the crosswalk and let them pass.

ALWAYS look for pedestrians who may be approaching the crosswalk or intersection before making a right turn.

### Intersections

Not all intersections require ALL cars to stop.

Some intersections have a 4-way stop, while others have a 2-way or 1-way stop.

If you come to an intersection with a ***4-way stop***, that means all cars must stop at the intersection.

If two cars arrive at the intersection at the same time, the car on the right gets to go first.

### Roundabouts & Traffic Circles

When approaching a roundabout or traffic circle, yield to any pedestrians or cyclists crossing the road.

Yield to any vehicles that are already in the roundabout before entering.

### Entering the Freeway

When merging onto a highway or freeway, oncoming traffic has the right-of-way.

The ideal speed for merging onto a highway or freeway is ***at or near the flow of traffic.***

### Funeral Processions

If you encounter a funeral procession, wait for the procession line to pass before driving.

### Constructions Zones

When driving through a construction zone, obey the posted speed limit and ***increase your following distance*** in case the car ahead of you slows or stops suddenly.

### Disabled Vehicles

If you see a vehicle stopped on the side of the road, the best thing to do is to slow down and move over into the left lane if you can. If you cannot change lanes, use extra caution when passing.

# COMMUNICATING WITH OTHER DRIVERS

## Using Your Horn

You should only use your horn when it is necessary to alert other drivers to potentially dangerous situations.

## Emergency Signals

If you see a crash ahead or some other potentially dangerous hazard (i.e., debris in the road), slow down, turn on your emergency flashers to alert other drivers coming up behind you.

If you need to pull off to the side of the road to stop, you should also turn on your flashers to let other drivers know that you are parked.

## Tapping Your Brakes

Tapping your brakes quickly several times in a row is also a good way to alert other drivers that there is danger up ahead or that you may need to slow down quickly.

For example, if you are driving on a highway and notice that traffic is stopped on the road ahead, tap your brakes lightly several times in a row to get the attention of the driver behind you and communicate that you will be slowing down quickly or stopping soon. This can help prevent a rear end collision.

### Flashing Your Headlights

There may be times when you or another driver wishes to yield the right-of-way.

For example, if you come to an intersection at the same time as another car, but want to let them to go first, you can flash your headlights quickly to let them know that you are giving them the right-of-way.

### Things to Avoid

You may encounter situations while driving that make you feel frustrated or angry. Always avoid communicating or behaving aggressively toward other drivers as this can increase your chances of being involved in a collision.

This includes things like making obscene hand gestures, honking the horn continuously (especially when stuck in traffic), flashing your high-beam headlights behind another driver, or following too closely.

Try to remain calm at all times while driving.

If you start to feel frustrated, roll down the window to get some fresh air and take a few deep breaths to calm down and clear your mind.

## PARKING

### Parking On a Hill

When parking with your car facing ***downhill***, turn your front wheels into the curb or toward the side of the road.

When parking with your car facing ***uphill***, turn your front wheels away from the curb and let the car roll back a few inches so that the wheels are gently touching the curb.

ALWAYS set the parking brake when you park on a hill, regardless of whether you are facing uphill or downhill. This prevents the car from rolling.

### Parallel Parking

When you parallel park, your vehicle should be no more than ***18 inches from the curb*** or edge of the road.

Pull your car up alongside the space in front of where you intend to park and stop when your rear bumper is in line with the front of the space.

Check your rearview mirror and look over your shoulder to make sure no cars are coming before you begin backing into the space.

### Parking At Painted Curbs

You can only park next to a ***white*** painted curb if you are picking up or dropping off passengers or mail.

You may NOT stop or park in front of a ***red*** painted curb at anytime.

You can only park in front of a ***blue*** painted curb if you are disabled and have a special placard or license plate.

### No Parking

It is ALWAYS illegal to park:

- If there is a "No Parking" sign,
- In a crosswalk, or
- When you are blocking a driveway, sidewalk, or ramp for disabled persons.

You may never park closer than ***15 feet*** from a fire hydrant.

You cannot park or stop closer than ***7 feet*** from a railroad track.

NEVER park your car in the street next to a vehicle parked legally at the curb. This is called "*double parking*."

Any vehicle parked on a California freeway for more than ***4 hours*** may be removed.

### Backing Up

When backing out of a parking space or driveway, turn and look over your right and left shoulders before you start backing up.

Do not rely solely on your mirrors.

# IDENTIFYING HAZARDOUS CONDITIONS

### Curved Roads

It can be difficult to see what's on the road ahead when the road curves.

The inertia or force of going around a curve can pull your car closer to the edge and away from the center of the road, making it easier to lose control of your vehicle, especially when the weather is bad.

### Wet Roads

When the road is wet, you should drive ***5 to 10 mph*** slower than you normally would.

NEVER slam on your brakes if there is water on the road. You could hydroplane and lose control of your vehicle.

**Roads are the most slippery right after it starts to rain**, especially if it hasn't rained recently. This is because the rainwater mixes with oil and dirt on the road to create a slick surface.

***Hydroplaning*** can occur whenever the road is wet from rain, snow, or a spill. When you hydroplane, your tires lose contact with the road, and you will be riding on top of the water. This causes you to lose traction and makes it very difficult to control your vehicle.

If you start to hydroplane, you should NOT hit the brakes. Instead, take your foot off the gas pedal and allow the vehicle to slow down gradually.

**Snow & Ice Covered Roads**

When the road is covered with snow, ***reduce your speed by half.***

When the road is icy, you should slow down to a crawl.

**Windy Conditions**

When it is windy, pay special attention to large vehicles driving near you, like semi-trucks and campers, since they can be moved easily by the wind.

**Fog & Smoke**

When heavy fog or smoke reduces visibility, AVOID driving if you can, or pull over until the fog lifts.

If you must drive, turn on your emergency flashers, go slowly, and use extra caution.

When visibility is reduced, you should increase the distance between you and the vehicle in front of you.

**Flooded Roads**

If you come to a flooded road, turn around and look for an alternate route.

NEVER drive through a flooded area if you can avoid it.

Flooded roadways can be life-threatening because it can be difficult to tell how deep the water is.

If you drive through water, your brakes could get wet. This can cause them to fail. After going through the water, test your brakes immediately before you continue to drive.

## EMERGENCY SITUATIONS

### Car Trouble

If you have car trouble while driving on the highway, turn on your emergency flashers and pull off the road as far away from oncoming traffic as possible.

### Handling Skids

If your vehicle starts to skid on the road, do not hit the brake.

Instead, take your foot off the accelerator and ***turn the wheel in the direction of the skid*** until you regain control.

### Drifting Off Road

If your vehicle drifts off the pavement, gently tap the brake to slow down gradually.

Check behind you and to your sides to ensure no cars are coming, then gently steer your vehicle back onto the road.

### Accelerator Malfunction

If your accelerator (gas pedal) malfunctions or becomes stuck, stay calm and shift the car into neutral.

Apply the brakes to slow down and look for a place to pull over.

**Do NOT turn off the engine while the vehicle is moving.**

NEVER reach down to look for objects on the ground while the car is moving.

### Brake Malfunction

If your brakes are not working correctly, shift the car into neutral and turn on your emergency flashers to alert other drivers that your vehicle has a problem.

Let the car slow down gradually and guide it to a safe spot off the road as soon as you can.

# SECTION 3: DRIVING LAWS

### Insurance & Registration

All vehicles must be registered and insured to drive on public roadways in the United States.

### Headlights

If you are driving ***after sunset*** or ***before sunrise***, you must turn on your low-beam headlights.

It is against the law to leave your high-beam headlights on when you are approaching another vehicle.

You are required by law to turn on your low-beam headlights when you enter a road construction zone.

### School Buses

If a school bus stops ahead of you and turns on its flashing red lights, you are legally required to stop and wait until the lights stop flashing before you continue to drive.

## Law Enforcement Stops

If a police car turns on its siren behind you, turn on your right turn signal to let the officer know that you see them and that you intend to stop.

Next, look for a safe place to pull over.

When an officer is approaching your vehicle for a traffic stop, roll down your window and place your hands on the steering wheel or in your lap so that the officer can see them.

## Traffic Tickets

If you are issued a traffic citation, you must appear in court if you wish to dispute the ticket, or you must pay a fine.

If you ignore a ticket by failing to show up to court or pay your fine on time, your license can be suspended.

## Collisions

Even if you are involved in a minor collision, you must stop to check on the other driver and exchange information.

If you are involved in a collision where someone is injured or killed, you must make a written report to the police.

## Alcohol

In most states, the legal limit is a BAC of 0.08%.

## Headphones

It is illegal to wear headphones or earplugs in both ears when driving because you cannot hear what is happening around you.

### Transporting Items

It is illegal to transport any items that block your view of the road or to the sides of your vehicle.

### Seatbelts

Most state laws require all passengers to wear a seatbelt when they are riding in a moving car.

### Bike Lanes

You can only drive in a bike lane if you are within **200 feet** of a cross street where you plan to turn right.

You may NOT drive in a bike lane at any other time.

### Flaggers

If there is a person directing traffic, you should follow their instructions at all times, even if they conflict with existing signs or signals.

### Crosswalks

It is illegal to park your vehicle in any crosswalk, whether marked or unmarked.

### Blocking An Intersection

It is ALWAYS illegal to block an intersection.

# SECTION 4: TRAFFIC LIGHTS & ROAD SIGNS

# TRAFFIC SIGNALS

In this section, you'll learn about the different types of traffic lights, signals and signs that control how you move when you are driving.

It is important that you understand the meaning of each one of these signs and signals, so that you know what to do when you see them out on the road.

## Traffic Lights & Arrows

Traffic signal lights control the movement of both vehicles and pedestrians.

### Red Lights — STOP

*STEADY RED LIGHT* - When you see a steady red light, STOP before the painted white line on the pavement.

If there is no line, stop before you enter the intersection.

Wait for the light the change to green before proceeding across the intersection.

You can turn ***right*** when the light is red, UNLESS there is a NO TURN ON RED sign.

If you are turning ***left***, stop first and yield to pedestrians and other traffic before making your turn.

*FLASHING RED LIGHT* - this should be treated like a ***stop sign***.

After making a complete stop, you can proceed once you have the right-of-way.

*STEADY RED ARROW* - this means STOP.

You may NOT make a turn at a red arrow.

Do not go until the arrow turns green.

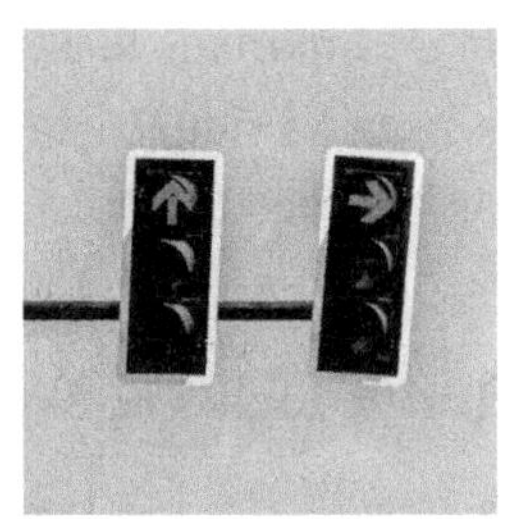

**Yellow Lights — CAUTION**

*STEADY YELLOW LIGHT* — this is a warning light that lets you know that the traffic signal is about to turn red.

If you see a yellow light, slow down and prepare to stop.

If you are in the intersection or cannot stop safely before entering the intersection, you may proceed through the intersection.

Never stop in the middle of an intersection or stop too suddenly. This can increase your chances of being involved in a collision.

*FLASHING YELLOW LIGHT* - means proceed with caution.

Slow down before you get to the intersection.

You do not need to stop for a yellow light that is blinking.

Be sure to yield to pedestrians, bicyclists, or other vehicles that are already in the intersection.

**Green Lights - GO**

A GREEN LIGHT means you can drive through the intersection if it is clear.

You may also turn right or left, but you must yield to other vehicles and pedestrians who are entering the intersection.

Remember to look both ways before crossing an intersection to make sure no other cars are coming EVEN IF you have a green light. Some drivers may not be paying attention.

*STEADY GREEN ARROW* - This signal means that you may turn in the direction of the arrow.

When there is no light on the arrow, you must yield to pedestrians and other cars before turning in that direction.

***What to do if traffic lights aren't working?***

There may be times when traffic lights and signals are not working.

They could lose power after a storm or they could be turned off because of construction in the area.

When traffic signal lights are ***not*** working, they should be treated as a STOP sign.

**Pedestrian Signals**

Some intersections have signal lights that let pedestrians know when it is safe to cross the intersection and when it is not.

*Walk Sign* - This signal light is shown when it is safe for pedestrians to cross the intersection.

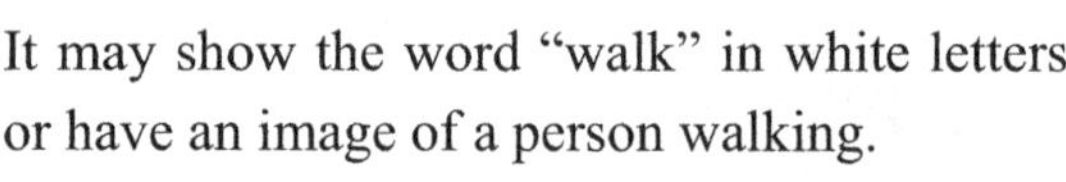

It may show the word "walk" in white letters or have an image of a person walking.

*Don't Walk* - This signal lets pedestrians know that it is not safe to cross the intersection and that they must wait for the signal to change before proceeding.

The signal light will show a solid raised hand with the words "don't walk."

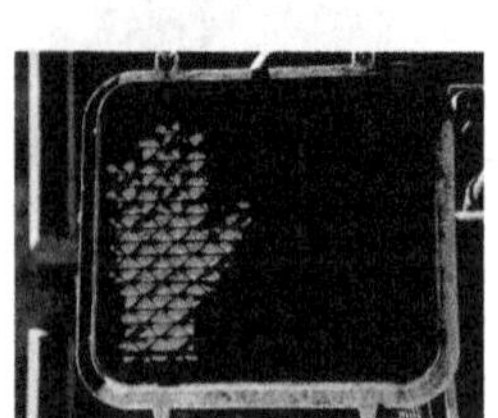

*Warning* - When a pedestrian signal is FLASHING the raised hand symbol or the words "don't walk," this is a warning that the traffic light is about to change.

Pedestrians that have not started crossing the intersection when the light begins to flash should wait until the light changes and the "walk" sign appears.

Pedestrians who are in the intersection when the light begins to flash should move out of the intersection quickly so that vehicles can cross safely once the light changes.

**Lane Control Signals**

Some highways have special signals over the lanes.

They are often used at:

- toll booths,
- multi-lane highways,
- bridges, and
- tunnels.

**This is what the different colors and symbols mean.**

GREEN ARROW - When you see a green arrow over a traffic lane, it means you CAN use the lane.

*STEADY RED X* - if you see this light over a traffic lane it means that you are NOT allowed to use the lane.

*STEADY YELLOW X* - This signal lets you know that the direction of the lane is changing soon. Move into another lane as soon as it is safe to do so.

*STEADY WHITE ONE-WAY LEFT-TURN ARROW* - if you see this arrow over your lane it means that you may only turn left if you are in that lane.

*STEADY WHITE TWO-WAY LEFT-TURN ARROW* - you may ONLY turn left if you are in this lane. However, this lane is also used by left-turning drivers who are approaching from the opposite direction.

# ROAD SIGNS

When you come to an intersection with a STOP sign you must stop completely.

**4-Way Stops**

Some intersections have stop signs placed in all four directions. This means that traffic coming from any direction must stop at the intersection.

**1 or 2-Way Stops**

Some intersections only have stop signs for one or two directions (for example, north and south) while traffic going east and west does NOT have to stop.

If you have a stop sign, but oncoming traffic does not, you must stop and wait for all traffic to clear before entering the intersection.

---

When you see a YIELD SIGN you must slow down and check for oncoming traffic.

If there is NO oncoming traffic, you do NOT have to stop.

If there is oncoming traffic, you must stop and wait for it to pass before proceeding.

---

These signs are posted at one-way streets and ramps entering or exiting a highway.

If you see this sign, do NOT enter the street or ramp in the direction you are driving.

---

When you see a one-way traffic sign it means that vehicles are only allowed to travel in the direction the sign is pointing.

Do not drive the wrong way down a one-way street, ramp, or lane.

---

Speed limit signs let you know the **maximum speed** you are allowed to drive on the road you are traveling on.

Keep in mind that **California's Basic Speed Limit Law** says that you should NEVER drive faster than is appropriate for conditions, regardless of the posted speed limit.

---

This sign lets you know that the road you are on intersects with a divided highway.

A ***divided highway*** is two, one-way lanes that are separated by a median or guide rail.

---

This sign lets you know that large trucks and tractor trailers are not allowed to use the road or drive on the highway.

---

This sign lets you know that bicycles are not allowed to ride on the road or highway because it is not safe for cyclists to travel on.

---

This sign lets you know that people are not allowed to cross the intersection on foot. They must go to another intersection where crossing is permitted.

---

This sign lets you know that you cannot make a U-turn.

A U-turn is when you make a 180-degree turn to go in the opposite direction.

---

This sign lets you know that right turns are prohibited at this intersection.

---

This sign lets you know left turns are not allowed at this intersection.

---

You cannot park your car in areas where a "no parking" sign is posted.

---

This sign lets you know that you are in a no passing zone. This means you are not allowed to pass vehicles traveling in the same direction as you.

---

This sign lets you know that traffic in the left lane must turn left at the intersection. However, traffic in the adjoining lane can turn left or continue driving straight.

---

This sign lets you know that the center lane can only be used by vehicles that are making left turns in either direction.

---

This sign lets you know that the roadway splits up ahead. If you are in the left lane, you must turn left. If you are in the right lane, you must turn right.

Make sure that you are in the correct lane depending on which direction you want to travel.

---

This sign lets you know that you have the option of continuing to drive straight or make a right turn from the lane you are driving in.

---

This sign lets you know that your lane must turn right at the intersection.

---

This sign lets you know that your lane must turn left at the intersection.

If you do not want to make a turn, you should move into another lane before you reach the intersection.

---

This sign lets you know that you need to stay to the right of a traffic island or divider.

These signs are often posted at the beginning of a divided highway.

---

This sign lets you know that a traffic light signal controls right turns at the intersection ahead.

---

This sign lets you know that you may not make a turn in either direction while the traffic light is red.

You must wait for the signal to turn green before proceeding.

---

This sign lets you know that you can make a left turn at the intersection, but you must yield to oncoming traffic and proceed only when you have enough space to make your turn safety.

---

This sign means that this is a parking space that is reserved for disabled people.

You must have an authorized license place or placard in order to park in a reserved parking spot.

If you are not authorized to park here, your vehicle may be towed and you will get a fine.

---

These signs let you know that you are in a school zone.

Slow down and be on the lookout for children.

You must yield to students who are crossing the street.

---

This type of sign warns you that there is a sharp change in the direction of the road ahead.

The road bends in the direction that the chevron arrow points. Slow down and use caution so that you do not lose control of your vehicle.

---

This left curve sign warns you that the road ahead veers to the left.

You may need to slow down to stay in your lane as you go around the curve.

---

This sign warns you that there is a sharp left turn in the road ahead. This is much more severe than a left curve. You should slow down and prepare to turn.

---

This sign warns you that the road ahead curves to the right. You may need to slow down so that you are able to stay in your lane as you go around the curve.

---

This sign warns you that the road ahead turns sharply to the right. You should slow down and prepare to turn.

Some signs have a reduced speed limit posted on the sign. You must not go faster than the posted limit when you approach the turn.

---

This sign lets you know that there is a set of curves in the road ahead.

The road may curve first in one direction, then curve back in the opposite direction.

The direction or shape of the curves will be indicated on the sign.

---

This sign lets you know that there are three or more curves in a row on the road ahead.

You should slow down and use extra caution until you get through the curves to avoid losing control of your vehicle.

---

This sign is used to warn you that the road changes at an extreme angle in the direction the arrow is pointing.

Slow down enough that you do not leave your lane as you go around the turn.

---

This sign warn you that trucks that go too fast around the curve risk tipping or rolling over.

Even if you are not driving a truck, you should be on the lookout for trucks that are driving near you. Give them extra space by slowing down or passing them.

Do not drive beside them while going around the curve. If they rollover or lose control, you could be involved in a fatal collision.

---

Advisory speed signs are special speed limit signs that tell you the maximum speed you can go when traveling around a curve or turn.

Driving faster than the recommended speed could result in a crash.

Once you pass the curve or turn, you can drive at the normal speed limit again if road conditions are good.

---

This sign is used to warn you that cars may be merging into your lane from a on-ramp or another roadway.

---

This sign lets you know that two roadways will meet ahead and travel in parallel lanes.

Traffic from the adjoining roadway does not have to merge since they use a new lane.

---

This sign is used to warn drivers that they are approaching an area where some traffic is entering the roadway, while other traffic is exiting.

This is often referred to as a "*weave area.*"

This means that many cars may be changing lanes around you and potentially crossing your path.

You should use extra caution in weave areas and pay close attention to what the vehicles around you are doing.

---

This sign lets you know that you are entering a divided highway.

A divided highway has two one-way roads with a divider or median between them.

You must stay on the RIGHT side of the median when you are driving onto a divided highway.

This sign is used on one-way streets that turn into two-lane roadways.

It lets you know that the one-way street that you are on is turning into a road with two lanes of traffic moving in opposite directions.

You should stay to the right to avoid colliding with oncoming traffic.

This sign is used on roads that have multiple lanes that are traveling in the same direction. It lets you know that the right lane is ending up ahead.

If you are in the right lane, you should turn on your left turn signal and move into the left lane as soon as it is safe to do so.

---

This sign lets you know that the left lane of a multi-lane roadway is ending.

If you are in the left lane, you should turn on your right turn signal and move into the right lane as soon as it is safe to do so.

---

This sign lets you know that two roads cross over each other at the intersection ahead.

Crossroads are often 4-way stops, but not always.

Pay close attention to the stop signs at the intersection so that you know who has the right of way if there is no traffic light.

If it is a 2-way stop, traffic crossing the intersection may not have to stop.

---

This sign lets you know that a road intersects the street you are driving on from one side only.

You should be on the lookout for cars turning onto the roadway from the side road, especially if there is no stop sign or traffic light controlling the intersection.

---

This sign lets you know that you will need to turn right or left at the intersection ahead.

Stop and look both ways before making your turn, especially if the intersection is not controlled by a traffic light.

---

This sign lets you know that the road splits into a Y shape with another road intersecting it.

---

This sign lets you know that there is a traffic circle ahead.

Traffic circles are used to slow down the flow of traffic when there are multiple turns or exits from a single roadway.

When you come to a traffic circle, yield to vehicles that are already in the circle before entering.

Use your turn signal to let other drivers know when and where you plan to exit the circle.

---

A large arrow that points in both directions lets you know that you must make a sharp right or left turn ahead.

This sign is often placed at the far side of a T-Intersection to let you know that the road does not continue going straight ahead.

---

This is a warning sign that lets you know that there is a bridge or overpass ahead.

When you approach the bridge or overpass, your lane will become more narrow.

You may need stop and wait before entering the bridge or overpass if there is a large or wide vehicle approaching, as there may not be enough room for both vehicles to pass each other without colliding.

---

This sign is used to warn you that the road may become very slippery when it rains or snows.

Keep in mind that roads are the most slippery when they first become wet because water mixes with oil and dirt on the road to create a slick surface.

It is very easy for your tires to slip and lose traction if you are driving too fast when this happens.

If the road is wet, slow down and and keep a safe distance from other cars on the road. That way, if you or another driver skids on the road-way, you'll both have more time to react and avoid a collision.

---

This sign warns you that deer are known to cross in the area. Slow down and drive with caution.

---

This sign is often posted at or near tunnels, overpasses, or parking garages. It lets you know the structure has a low ceiling.

If your vehicle is taller than the height listed on the sign, you should not enter.

---

This sign lets you know that the shoulder of the road is lower than the level of the road. In some cases, there could be as much as a 3-inch drop from the road to the shoulder.

This difference can cause you to lose control of your car if one wheel strays onto the shoulder, so use extra caution in these areas.

---

This sign lets you know that there is a steep hill ahead. You should slow down before going down the hill to stay in control of you car.

Avoid "riding" or overusing your brakes when driving down a steep grade. Rather, tap the brakes periodically to reduce your speed on a hill if you need to.

---

This sign lets you know that there is a traffic light at the intersection ahead.

You should slow down when you see this sign because there could be a line of vehicles stopped ahead, or the light could be red when you get to the intersection.

---

This sign lets you know that there is a stop sign ahead.

When you see this sign, slow down and prepare to stop.

---

This sign lets you know that bicycles frequently cross the road in this area or at this intersection.

Slow down and be prepared to stop to avoid causing injury to a cyclist.

---

This sign lets you know that there are railroad tracks ahead that you will need to cross over.

You should start looking down the tracks and listening for trains that may be approaching as soon as you see this sign.

---

This sign lets you know that there is a crosswalk ahead where pedestrians walk.

You should slow down and prepare to stop if any pedestrians are trying to cross the street.

Always look back to your right and check for pedestrians who may be entering the crosswalk before making a right turn. They can be hard to see, especially if you are driving at night.

---

This sign is used in areas where horse drawn vehicles such as buggies, carts, or carriages are known to use the road regularly.

Try to give these vehicles extra space if you can and use caution when you pass them. Driving too close to horses or honking your horn at them can spook them and cause them to lose control.

Road work signs let you know that there is road construction ahead. If the light on the sign is flashing, that means that it is an active worksite and there may be people working on or near the road.

You should start to slow down and be on the lookout for additional signs or flaggers that may redirect you through the work zone.

Work zone signs let you know when you are entering or leaving an active road construction zone.

Active work zones usually contain more potential hazards that you need to watch out for, such as workers, construction vehicles, and other equipment.

There may also be dust or smoke from the construction that may make it difficult to see clearly.

Always turn on your headlights when you enter an active construction zone and use extra caution to avoid collisions with people or equipment.

---

When road work is being done, it is common for one or more lanes of traffic to be closed. This type of sign lets you know that the right lane of traffic is closed ahead.

When you see a sign like this, you should turn on your signal and merge into the lane that is open as soon as it is safe to do so.

---

This sign lets you know that there are people working very close to the road up ahead.

When you see this sign, slow down, stay alert, and use extra caution to avoid hitting or injuring a road worker.

---

This sign lets you know that there is a human flagger ahead that is directing traffic.

Stay alert and be prepared to stop or slow down. Always follow the flagger's instructions.

---

This sign lets you know that the road is closed due to flooding. If you see this sign, do NOT drive on the road. Turn around and find another route.

Driving through water on flooded roads is very dangerous and can be life threatening.

---

Barrels, cones, tubes and panels are often used in road construction zones to direct traffic to an alternate lane or keep traffic out of certain areas.

You should always treat channeling devices like a barrier. Do not drive through them or knock them over. They are there for your safety and the protection of the road workers.

---

Highway guide signs are used to let you know about upcoming exits to cities or connecting highways and roads.

These signs are usually green with white lettering and will tell you how far away your exit is (i.e. 1 mile)

Highway guide signs that include a yellow "EXIT ONLY" sign with an arrow, let you know that you are in an exit lane. If you stay in this lane, you must exit the highway.

Exits can be on the right or left side of the highway. The placement of the exit number will let you know what side the exit is on. There will usually be arrows pointing in the direction of the exit as well.

---

Interstate highways are roads that travel through more than one state. These signs are blue and red with white lettering.

Interstates run east to west or north to south. Interstate signs usually say which direction you are heading. For example, the sign in the image lets you know that you are traveling east on I-40.

---

This type of guide sign lets you know that services such hospitals, food, gas or hotels are available in the area, or they will indicate how far away they are.

These signs are usually blue with white lettering or images.

---

This type of sign is used to direct drivers to local attractions like state parks, museums, and rest areas. These signs are usually blue, brown or green with white lettering.

# SECTION 5: Q&A

# PRACTICE QUESTIONS & EXPLANATIONS

**Question 1: If a school bus stops ahead of you and turns on its flashing red lights, you are legally required to:**

A. Stop and wait until the lights stop flashing before continuing to drive.

B. Pass the bus on the left.

C. Go around the bus on the right if you have enough room.

**The correct answer is A.** If a school bus stops ahead of you and turns on its flashing red lights, you are legally required to stop and wait until the lights stop flashing before you continue to drive.

**Question 2: If a police car turns on its siren behind you, you should:**

A. Continue driving until you reach a public parking lot.

B. Stop immediately in the middle of the road.

C. Turn on your right turn signal and look for a safe place to pull over.

**The correct answer is C.** If a police car turns on its siren behind you, you should turn on your right turn signal to let the officer know that you see them and intend to stop. Then, look for a safe place to pull over.

**Question 3: If you are issued a traffic citation, you must:**

A. Appear in court or pay a fine.

B. Make excuses or cry to get out of the ticket.

C. Offer money to the officer in exchange for canceling the ticket.

**The correct answer is A.** If you are issued a traffic citation, you must appear in court if you wish to dispute it or pay a fine.

**Question 4: If you are involved in a "fender bender" or minor collision:**

A. You don't need to stop if no one appears injured.

B. You must stop and exchange information with the other driver.

C. You don't need to stop if you hit a parked car with no passengers inside.

**The correct answer is B.** Even if you are involved in a minor collision, you must still stop to check on the other driver and exchange information.

**Question 5: You are required by law to _______ when entering a road construction zone.**

A. Honk the horn.

B. Turn on your low-beam headlights.

C. Turn on your high-beam headlights.

**The correct answer is B.** You are required by law to turn on your low-beam headlights when you enter a road construction zone.

**Question 6: It is illegal for anyone to operate a vehicle if their blood alcohol level (BAC) is _______ or higher.**

A. 0.08%

B. 0.05%

C. 0.03%

**The correct answer is A.** The legal limit is a BAC of 0.08%.

**Question 7: Which of the following increases your chances of being involved in a crash?**

A. Looking at your phone.

B. Driving when you are tired.

C. Both A and B.

**The correct answer is C.** Driving while you are tired or looking at your phone can increase your odds of getting into an accident.

**Question 8. How often should you check your tire pressure?**

A. Every three months.

B. At least once a month or before a long road trip.

C. Every six months.

**The correct answer is B**. You should check your tire pressure at least once a month or before going on a long car trip.

**Question 9: Unless otherwise posted, the speed limit in a school zone is:**

A. 55 mph

B. 25 mph

C. 5 mph

**The correct answer is B.** Unless otherwise posted, the speed limit in an active school zone is 25 mph.

**Question 10: *Managing space* is a defensive driving skill that involves:**

A. Understanding the meaning of road signs and signals.

B. Leaving enough room between you and the car in front of you or to the sides of you.

C. Knowing when to turn on your headlights.

**The correct answer is B.** "*Managing space*" is a defensive driving skill that involves leaving enough room between you and the car in front of you or to the sides of your vehicle.

**Question 11: One important fact to know about large trucks is:**

A. They take longer to stop than smaller passenger vehicles.

B. They can speed up quickly.

C. They can stop more quickly than smaller cars.

**The correct answer is A.** It is important to know that it takes large trucks longer to stop than smaller passenger vehicles. Therefore, if you slow down or stop quickly in front of a large truck, it could cause a collision.

**Question 12: If you are driving after sunset or before sunrise, you must:**

A. Turn on your windshield wipers.

B. Turn on your low-beam headlights.

C. Turn on your fog lights.

**The correct answer is B.** If you are driving after sunset or before sunrise, you must turn on your low-beam headlights.

**Question 13: A traffic signal with a steady red light means:**

A. You may turn left if there is no oncoming traffic.

B. You must stop at the white line or before the intersection if no line is present.

C. You must yield to oncoming traffic, but you do not have to stop if no one is coming.

**The correct answer is B.** If you come to a traffic signal with a steady red light, you must stop at the white line or before entering the intersection and wait until the light changes to green before proceeding.

**Question 14: When are you required to wear a seat belt?**

A. Any time you are driving faster than 25 mph.

B. Any time you are driving at any speed.

C. Only when driving on multi-lane highways.

**The correct answer is B**. Seatbelts are the law. Therefore, you (and your passengers) must wear a seatbelt anytime you are driving.

**Question 15: Why is it important to adjust the driver's seat?**

A. To make sure you'll be comfortable.

B. To be able to reach the pedals and see clearly out the windshield.

C. So that the person sitting behind you has enough legroom.

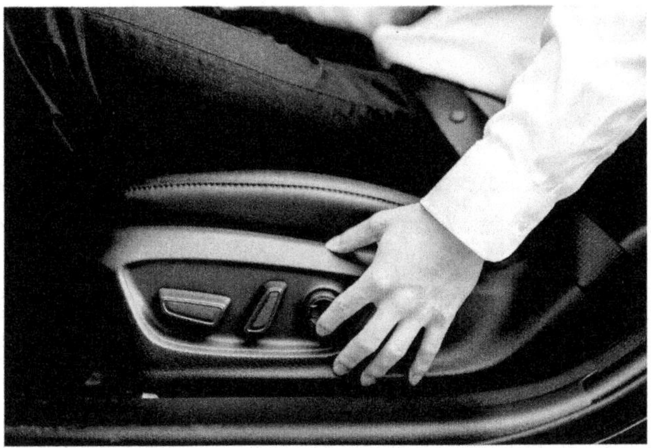

**The correct answer is B**. It is important to adjust your seat to reach the pedals and see clearly out the windshield easily.

**Question 16: The speed limit when driving through a blind intersection (with no stop sign or signal) is:**

A. 45 mph

B. 30 mph

C. 15 mph

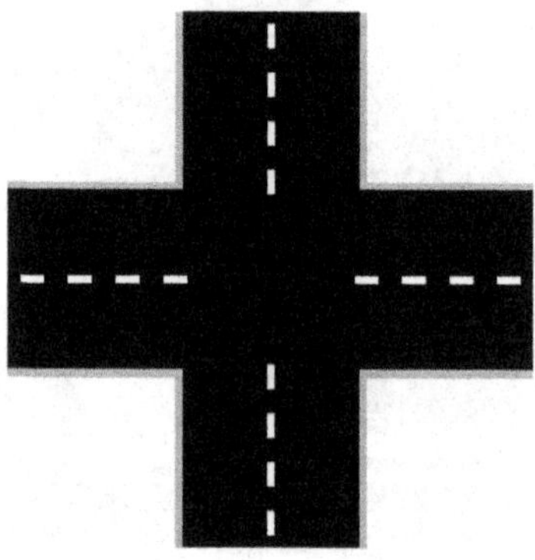

**The correct answer is C.** The speed limit when driving through a blind intersection is 15 mph.

**Question 17: When driving, you should:**

A. Fix your gaze on the center of the road immediately in front of you.

B. Constantly scan your surroundings for situations that could cause an accident.

C. Focus only on the car in front of you.

**The correct answer is B.** When you are driving, constantly scan your surroundings for potential dangers. This includes looking ahead 10-15 seconds, looking to the sides of your car, and checking your mirrors often to see what's going on around you.

**Question 18: A safe following distance in good driving conditions is:**

A. 1 second

B. 2 seconds

C. 4 seconds

**The correct answer is C.** A safe following distance in good driving conditions is 4 seconds. Remember to allow more space when the road or weather conditions are not ideal.

**Question 19: When you come to an intersection, you should look:**

A. Right, left, then right again before crossing.

B. Left, right, then left again before crossing.

C. Straight ahead if you have a green light.

**The correct answer is B.** When you come to an intersection, you should look left, right, and then back to your left again before crossing since traffic coming from the left will be closest to you.

Remember, just because you have a green light or the right-of-way does not mean that other drivers will always comply. They might be distracted or driving under the influence.

**Question 20: A blind spot is:**

A. An area of the road that is difficult to see because it is too far ahead of you.

B. A special crosswalk for blind pedestrians.

C. The area around a vehicle that a driver can't see in their rearview or side mirrors.

**The correct answer is C.** A blind spot is an area around a vehicle that a driver can't see in their rearview or side mirrors.

**Question 21: If you are driving 55 mph, how much space will you need to come to a complete stop?**

A. 100 feet

B. 250 feet

C. 400 feet

**The correct answer is C.** If you are going 55 mph, you will need 400 feet of space to come to a complete stop.

**Question 22: When a long vehicle, such as a tractor-trailer, makes a turn, the back wheels have a _______ path than those in the front.**

A. Longer.

B. Shorter.

C. The same length.

**The correct answer is B.** When long vehicles make turns, the back wheels have a shorter path than those in the front. This causes them to have to swing out wide when turning.

**Question 23: It is against the law to leave your high-beam headlights on when:**

A. You are driving in the daytime.

B. You are approaching another vehicle.

C. You are driving on a rural road.

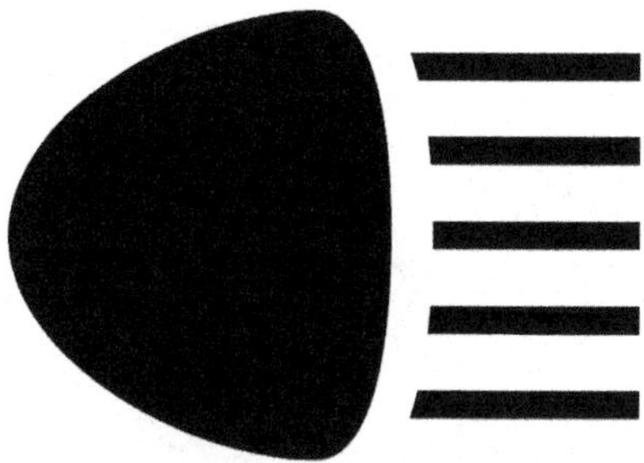

**The correct answer is B.** It is against the law to leave your high-beam headlights on when you are approaching another vehicle.

**Question 24: You can reduce the risk of carbon monoxide poisoning by**:

A. Never running the engine in a garage with the door closed.

B. Opening your car windows with you are parked outside with the engine running.

C. Both A and B.

**The correct answer is C.** You can reduce the risk of carbon monoxide poisoning by not running the engine in a garage when the door is closed and opening your car windows with you are parked outside with the engine running.

You should also have your exhaust system checked regularly for leaks.

**Question 25: The speed limit when driving near or crossing railroad tracks is ______ unless otherwise posted.**

A. 5 mph

B. 10 mph

C. 15 mph

**The correct answer is C.** Unless otherwise posted, the speed limit when driving near or crossing railroad tracks is 15 mph.

**Question 26: When driving in poor weather conditions:**

A. It takes longer to react and stop.

B. It takes the same amount of time to react and stop.

C. It takes less time to react and stop.

**The correct answer is A.** For example, when driving in poor weather conditions such as rain or fog, it takes longer to stop than when operating in perfect conditions.

**Question 27: When entering or merging onto the freeway, you should drive:**

A. At or near the same speed as the flow of traffic.

B. 25 mph slower than the flow of traffic.

C. Faster than the flow of traffic.

**The correct answer is A.** When entering the freeway, you should drive at or near the same speed as traffic flow. Going significantly faster or slower than the flow of traffic can increase your chances of causing a crash.

**Question 28: If you come to a safety zone where people are boarding or exiting a bus or trolley, you must:**

A. Drive through the safety zone at no more than 40 mph.

B. Stop and wait until all pedestrians are safely away from the road before you proceed.

C. Honk your horn as you drive through to let pedestrians know that they should wait to cross.

**The correct answer is B.** If you come to a safety zone where people are boarding or exiting a bus or trolley, you must stop and wait until all pedestrians are safely away from the road before you proceed.

**Question 29: Which type of vehicle must ALWAYS stop before crossing train tracks?**

A. School or city busses.

B. Truck that transport hazardous materials.

C. Both A and B.

**The correct answer is C.** Both busses and trucks transporting hazardous materials must always stop before crossing railroad tracks, regardless of whether there is a stop sign or signal.

**Question 30: You should stop at least _____ feet from the nearest railroad tracks when crossing devices such as lights are active or blinking.**

A. 15

B. 10

C. 5

**The correct answer is A.** You should stop at least 15 feet from (but no more than 50 feet) from the nearest railroad tracks when crossing devices, such as lights, are active or blinking.

**Question 31: If an emergency vehicle such as an ambulance, fire truck, or police car, is using its siren and lights, you must:**

A. Pull over and stop only if they are traveling in the same direction as you on a two-way street.

B. Pull over and stop if they are traveling in either direction on a two-way street.

C. Pull over and stop if they are on the opposite side of you on a divided highway.

**The correct answer is B.** If you are driving on a two-way street and you see an emergency vehicle using their siren and lights coming from either direction, you must pull over to the shoulder of the road and stop to give them room to get through.

**Question 32: If the car ahead of you is stopped at a crosswalk, you should:**

A. Slowly pass the vehicle on the left.

B. Never pass a vehicle that is stopped at a crosswalk.

C. Honk your horn so that they get out of your way.

**The correct answer is B.** You should never pass a vehicle that is stopped at a crosswalk. Someone could be crossing the street that you are not able to see.

**Question 33: If you come to an intersection with a 4-way stop, that means:**

A. All cars must stop at the intersection.

B. Only cars traveling east or west must stop at the intersection.

C. Only cars traveling north or south must stop at the intersection.

**The correct answer is A.** If you come to an intersection with a 4-way stop, that means all cars must stop at the intersection.

**Question 34: It is illegal to wear headphones ________ while driving.**

A. At all.

B. In one ear.

C. In both ears.

**The correct answer is C.** It is illegal to wear headphones or earplugs in both ears when driving because you cannot hear what is happening around you.

**Question 35: When are you allowed to drive in a bike lane?**

A. During rush hour traffic, if there are no bicyclists in the bike lane.

B. When you are within 200 feet of a cross street where you plan to turn right.

C. When you want to pass a driver ahead of you who is turning right.

**The correct answer is B.** You can drive in a bike lane if you are within 200 feet of a cross street where you plan to turn right.

**Question 36: If you see a signal person or "flagger" at a road construction site ahead, when should you obey their instructions?**

A. Only when you see orange cones on the road ahead.

B.. At all times, unless they conflict with existing signs or signals.

C. At all times, no matter what.

**The correct answer is C.** If there is a person directing traffic, you should follow their instructions at all times, even if they conflict with existing signs or signals.

**Question 37: When are you legally allowed to block an intersection?**

A. When you entered the intersection on the green light.

B. During rush hour traffic.

C. Under no circumstances.

**The correct answer is C.** It is always illegal to block an intersection.

**Question 38: When approaching a roundabout or traffic circle, you should always:**

A. Yield to pedestrians or cyclists crossing the road.

B. Yield to any vehicles that are already in the circle.

C. Both A and B.

**The correct answer is C.** When approaching a roundabout or traffic circle, you should yield to any pedestrians or cyclists crossing the road. You should also yield to any vehicles that are already in the roundabout before entering.

**Question 39: It is illegal to park your vehicle:**

A. In an unmarked crosswalk.

B. Within three feet of a private driveway.

C. In a bike lane.

**The correct answer is A.** It is illegal to park your vehicle in an unmarked crosswalk.

**Question 40: When driving behind a motorcycle, you should keep a _____ second following distance between them and you.**

A. 1

B. 2

C. 4

**The correct answer is C.** When driving behind a motorcycle, you should keep a 4-second following distance.

This way, if the motorcycle stops suddenly or skids, you have a better chance of avoiding a collision.

Made in the USA
Middletown, DE
12 January 2023

21999762R10086